Marketplace

Money Matters

An Introduction to Economics

Barbara Gottfried Hollander

Heinemann Library
Chicago, Illinois

www.heinemannraintree.com
Visit our website to find out
more information about
Heinemann-Raintree books.

To order:
☎ Phone 888-454-2279
🖥 Visit www.heinemannraintree.com
to browse our catalog and order online.

Edited by Adam Miller and Andrew Farrow
Designed by Ryan Frieson
Original illustrations © Capstone Global Library
  Ltd 2011
Illustrated by Planman Technologies (India) Pvt
  Ltd
Maps by Mapping Specialists, Ltd
Picture research by Hannah Taylor

Originated by Capstone Global Library Ltd
Printed and bound in China by South China
  Printing Company Ltd

15 14 13 12 11 10
9 8 7 6 5 4 3 2 1

**Library of Congress Cataloging-in-Publication
Data**
Hollander, Barbara, 1970-
  Money matters : an introduction to economics /
Barbara Hollander.
     p. cm.—(The global marketplace)
  Includes bibliographical references and index.
  ISBN 978-1-4329-3929-8 (hc)
  1. Economics. 2. Money. I. Title.
HB171.H668 2011
  330—dc22   2010003996

Acknowledgments

The author and publisher are grateful to the
following for permission to reproduce copyright
material: Alamy Images pp. **8** (© Oleksiy
Maksymenko Photography), **18** (© vario images
GmbH & Co.KG), **34** (© Jim West); Corbis pp. **11**
(Tim Pannell), **17** (Randy Faris), **21** (Reuters/Mark
Wilson), **23** (Andrew Holbrooke), **33** (Reuters/
Philimon Bulawayo), **45** (Reuters/Mohamed
Nureldin); Getty Images pp. **5** (Stone), **19** (Mario
Tama), **24** (LOOK/Annie Engel), **26** (Peter
Macdiarmid), **28** (Bruno Vincent), **36** (Bloomberg
News/Si Barber), **39** (Yann Layma), **46** (AFP/
Vanderlei Almeida); istockphoto pp. **6** (© Uygar
Ozel), **15** (© Ed O'Neil), **42**.

Cover photograph of a glass globe resting on a
variety of different currencies reproduced with
permission of istockphoto (© redmal).

We would like to thank Michael Miller and
Laura J. Hensley for their invaluable help in the
preparation of this book.

Every effort has been made to contact copyright
holders of any material reproduced in this book.
Any omissions will be rectified in subsequent
printings if notice is given to the publisher.

All the Internet addresses (URLs) given in this book
were valid at the time of going to press. However,
due to the dynamic nature of the Internet, some
addresses may have changed, or sites may have
changed or ceased to exist since publication. While
the author and publisher regret any inconvenience
this may cause readers, no responsibility for any
such changes can be accepted by either the author
or the publisher.

Contents

Some words are printed in bold, **like this**. You can find out what they mean by looking in the glossary.

Why Economics Matters

Sometimes a little knowledge can save the world—and a lack of knowledge can cause big problems. In the case of **economics**, the study of how we can use our limited **resources** to meet our many needs, many believe that a little knowledge could have prevented a big crisis that occurred in recent history.

A good deal?

Put yourself in the shoes of someone buying a home in 2005. Houses are getting so expensive that you know you cannot afford one—and you worry that houses will only keep getting more expensive. Yet everyone around you seems to be buying a home. Then, someone from a bank offers to lend you money to buy a home at a low **interest rate**, or cost of borrowing. Some people tell you that you will be able to resell the house for a big **profit** in the next few years. So, you jump at the opportunity.

But if you had known a little about economics, you would not have bought the home. You would have known that the high home **prices** would eventually come down. In other words, you would have seen that you would be paying too much for the house. And you would have known that your **loan** (the money you borrowed) would soon become much more expensive to pay back—and, if you could not afford the monthly payments, you could find yourself forced out of your new home and on the street.

Where does *economics* come from?

The word *economics* comes from the Greek word *oikonomos*, which means "one who manages a household." In a sense, the household was the first **economy**. Long ago, most people had farms. They used natural resources such as the land and trees to grow food, build homes, and provide heat. People even used their animals for food and clothing. So, people used their resources to make the **goods** and **services** needed to live.

Later, people began to specialize in one job. They realized that they could make one item and then trade it for something else that they wanted. For example, a person could raise sheep and then trade the sheep's wool for other goods. Soon, this system involved money. People could bring their goods to marketplaces and exchange them for money. Then, they could use this money to buy other goods.

Decisions add up

Thousands of times in the 2000s, people made bad economic decisions like this and bought homes they could not afford. When these people could not afford to pay back the banks, everyone got nervous. Soon the banks themselves were having trouble paying back the money they had borrowed to offer the loans in the first place. The whole financial system seemed to be collapsing.

It took a lot of people with knowledge about economics to prevent an even worse disaster. Even so, the crisis affected millions of people. Companies shut down, and millions of people lost their jobs. People had trouble paying their bills. People's individual economic decisions had lasting effects on people around the world.

WHAT IT MEANS TO ME   How does it affect you?

But how does all of this affect you? In your everyday life, you are faced with basic economic decisions. For example, you may want to see both a new movie and buy a new CD. But you can only afford to spend your money on one option or the other. If you pick the movie, you lose the music. Based on your personal financial situation, you have to choose the option that is best for you.

As you get older, your decisions about economics will be even more important— as seen in the example of homebuyers in 2005 on page 4. By understanding economics, you will be able to make important decisions about your future, such as how much of a college loan you can afford, whether or not a certain credit card is a good idea, or what kind of business you should start for yourself. Read on to learn more about how economics works, and how economics affects your everyday life.

Whenever you decide whether or not to buy something, you are making an economic decision. Economics is about making choices.

Supply and Demand

You want to buy a new pair of jeans. So, you head to the store with money in your wallet. Once inside, you see rows of jeans. This selection is the **supply** that the store has to offer. You try on a few pairs, because you are willing and able to buy the jeans. In other words, you "**demand**" a new pair of jeans.

What is supply?

Supply is the amount, or **quantity**, of a good or service that a business produces and brings to the **market** for sale. Cars, computers, clothing, and food are examples of goods. Services are actions like getting a haircut or going to the doctor. Businesses can sell these products and make money.

Shocking, isn't it?

Supply shocks are unexpected events that cause businesses to change their supply. For example, supply shocks often come from the oil industry. Many industries rely on gasoline, which is made from oil, to transport their goods and to heat office buildings and factories.

When oil prices increase, it costs more money for businesses to make their goods. For example, a factory's heating bill will be higher each month. This means that businesses have to charge a higher price just to cover their costs. In 2003 a barrel of oil cost $32. But in May 2008 oil prices increased to about $130 a barrel. As a result, many businesses raised the prices of their products.

Rising oil prices increase the price of gasoline, making it more expensive for people to drive cars. It also increases the price of other products, because businesses use oil to power factories and ship goods.

Input costs

The main factor in deciding the quantity that will be supplied is the cost of the **inputs**. For example, the inputs for making cookies include flour, sugar, eggs, and oil, as well as the time of the baker. What if we wanted the baker to make one more cookie? What would that cost? This amount of money—the extra cost of producing one more cookie—is called the **marginal cost**.

Resources are a big part of a company's inputs. They are what businesses use to create things and grow. For example, human resources make up the labor force, or the people who work in a business. Natural resources come from nature, such as water, trees, coal, and petroleum. And **capital** resources are resources made by people, such as buildings and equipment.

But there is always a limit to resources. Because resources are limited, people and businesses have to make choices. These choices shape our economic system.

Making money

Both people and businesses have **income**. This is money that comes into their wallets and bank accounts. Money earned from working (known as salaries or wages) is an example of a person's income. Money made from selling goods is an example of a business's income.

Both people and businesses have **expenses**, too. Expenses are items that people and businesses pay for, such as a house, an office building, workers, and ingredients to make cookies. A business uses its **revenue**, or the money it makes, to pay for its expenses. Any money left over is called profit.

Choosing a price

Since making a profit depends on revenue and expenses, businesses usually choose a price for their product that is more than the cost of making the product. Businesses also like to make a lot of their products, because more sales can mean more profits. For example, if you ran a cookie business, you would likely earn more total profits if you sold 50 cookies than if you only sold 25 cookies.

Making the connection

In economics, there are laws, or rules, about how people and businesses usually behave. When a business can charge a higher price, it earns more money from each sale. Then, a business can use this extra money to make more products—and even more money. So, higher prices encourage businesses to make more products. This is known as the "law of supply."

What is demand?

Supply is only half of the economic story. Demand is just as important. Suppliers can always offer their goods and services, but **consumers** (the people who buy goods) must be willing and able to buy them. Otherwise, the new pairs of jeans will just stay on the shelves.

Consumers have wants and needs. A want is something that you would like to have. Wants are different than needs. A need is something that you must have in order to survive, such as air and water. Perhaps you do not need a new pair of jeans, but it would be nice to have them.

Price

Let's say you try on two pairs of jeans that look equally good on you. But one pair costs $30 and the other pair costs $115. Which one do you choose? You pick the pair that costs $30. Why spend an extra $85 to own a pair of jeans? You choose the pair of jeans that costs the least.

This example shows how price and demand are related. Price can cause people to demand products—or to not want them at all. For example, when the price of an item drops, more people usually want to buy it. And when an item becomes more expensive, then people will usually demand less of that item.

Price can also affect how many products a person will demand. For example, perhaps you would choose to buy two pairs of the $30 jeans in different styles because you can get more for your money.

When products become less expensive, more people usually want to buy them.

Income and tastes

A person's income affects what a person can afford. If people make more money, then they are able to buy more goods and services. And if people make less money, then they will have to change their spending habits and buy fewer goods.

Tastes, or preferences, also affect the demand for goods and services. For example, say a consumer is trying to decide between two cell phones. Both phones are made by the same company and have the same features. But the first phone is a dull gray and the other is metallic black. Even if the gray phone costs less, the consumer may still choose to buy the black phone because he or she prefers the way it looks.

Specific factors

Specific factors, such as population and climate, also influence demand. Generally, a place with more people (population) will mean there is a higher demand for goods and services. This is because there are more consumers to buy products. Different climates also affect the demand for certain products. For example, people demand more ski equipment in cold climates, but more swimsuits in warmer areas.

Prices of related goods

The prices of related goods affect demand, too. For example, gloves and mittens are **substitutes**. This means that they can replace one another. If the price of gloves rises, then the demand for gloves will fall. People will buy fewer gloves because they became more expensive. But people will buy more mittens because they now cost less compared to gloves. So, an increase in the price of a good leads to higher demand for its substitute.

GOODS AND THEIR COMPLEMENTS	
Goods	Complements
Ice cream	Ice cream cones
Tennis rackets	Tennis balls
Coffee beans	Coffee pots
Televisions	Cable TV service

Peanut butter and jelly are **complements**. They go together. What happens if the price of peanut butter goes up? Fewer people will buy peanut butter. In other words, the demand for peanut butter falls. But what happens to the demand for jelly? Since peanut butter and jelly go together, people now buy less jelly, too. So, an increase in the price of a good (such as peanut butter) leads to a decrease in the demand for both the good and its complement (such as jelly).

What do you consider elastic?

Which goods in your life are elastic, and which are inelastic? You can find the answer by asking yourself certain questions:

- If your family won the lottery, would you buy more food?

- If your family made less money, would you stop eating out in restaurants?

- Would you demand more ketchup, mustard, or relish if hot dog prices went down?

- Would you eat less popcorn if you stopped going to the movies?

- If you went to the store to get a new cell phone and found out it was going on sale next week, would you wait to buy the phone?

Price elasticity

As we have seen, the supply and demand of everything is affected by its price. But some goods are more affected by price than others.

Price elasticity is a measure of how sensitive supply and demand are to changes in price. If the demand or supply for a product is sensitive to a price change, then the product is called an **elastic** good. That means that a small fall in prices will lead to a large increase in the number of the product that people will buy.

Changes in the price of elastic goods will affect how many people buy those goods. For example, if prices go down on computers, the demand will probably increase.

What happens if the demand or supply of a product is affected very little by price changes? Then, the product is called **inelastic**.

Elasticity over time

Economists study the effects of **producer** and consumer behaviors in different time frames. The price elasticity of a good or service may change depending on the time frame.

The short run is a time frame in which only some economic factors change. The long run is a longer time frame in which all factors can change—for example, new businesses can open or older businesses can close down. In the long run, there is also time for consumers to change their spending habits. For example, by early 2008 oil prices began to rise. This led to higher gasoline prices. At first, U.S. consumers did not respond to the higher gas prices. Gas was fairly inelastic. But in the months ahead, as gas prices continued to rise, Americans responded by cutting down on their driving. By August 2008 the demand for oil in the United States had its largest six-month drop in 26 years.

Many medicines are inelastic goods, because people will buy them even if prices go up. For example, people need certain medicines to remain healthy, so they will pay whatever they need to pay.

The effect of income

If you won the lottery, what kind of things would you buy more of? What would you buy less of? Winning the lottery affects your income. Economists study how increases in income can change the demand for certain goods and services. This is called the income elasticity of demand.

If a person makes more money than he or she did before but demands less of a product, then the item is known as an **inferior good**. Bus travel is an example of an inferior good. As average income increases, people buy their own cars or take taxis or airplanes, rather than traveling by bus.

But if a person makes more money and buys more of a product, then the item is called a **normal good**. Cars, cell phones, and computers are all examples of normal goods. Normal goods can be both necessities (needs) and luxuries (wants). For example, food is a necessity that everyone buys. But if a person makes more money, then he or she might spend more on expensive groceries and restaurants. Expensive vacations and dishwashers are luxuries. A person with more money would feel free to spend money on these kinds of things.

Tables and graphs

Are you a person who needs to see things in order to understand them? Did you ever hear someone say, "A picture is worth a thousand words?" Economists use a lot of tools to see how people and businesses act, and sometimes they even try to predict the future.

Tables and graphs are two ways that economists see supply and demand. A table called a supply schedule shows you the quantity that will likely be supplied at different prices. So, let's look at the market for DVDs. How many DVDs will businesses supply? It depends on the price. A supply schedule gives you options.

SUPPLY SCHEDULE FOR A DVD	
Price (per DVD)	Quantity (of DVDs)
$5	0
$10	10
$15	30
$20	35
$25	50
$30	60

The supply schedule tells you that at $5, businesses should not bother making any DVDs, because they will not make much (if any) profit. But if the price is $30, then businesses would be motivated to make more DVDs. Now, 60 DVDs are available for sale. But can businesses sell a DVD for $30? Will people buy at that price? Let's look at the demand schedule.

DEMAND SCHEDULE FOR A DVD	
Price (per DVD)	Quantity (of DVDs)
$5	45
$10	40
$15	30
$20	20
$25	10
$30	0

The demand schedule tells you how many DVDs will be demanded (or bought) at each price. So, will people buy a DVD for $30? No, people will not demand any DVDs at a price of $30. But if the price drops to $25, then 10 DVDs will be sold. And at a price of $15, 30 DVDs will be sold. Look back at the supply schedule chart. At $15, 30 DVDs would also be supplied. This is called the equilibrium point. This is the point at which supply meets demand.

Laws and elasticity

The supply and demand schedules allow you to see economic laws and elasticity. Look again at the charts. Looking at the supply schedule chart, what happens to the quantity supplied as price increases? It goes up, because businesses can make more money. That is the law of supply. Looking at the demand schedule, what happens to the quantity demanded as price increases? It goes down, because as things become more expensive, people buy less (or not at all). That is the law of demand.

WHAT IT MEANS TO ME　　**Smart shopping**

Thinking about elasticity can help you be a smarter shopper. If what you want is inelastic (such as food), you might have to buy it now and not settle for a substitute, if your options are limited. You are willing to pay a higher price if necessary. But if a product you want is elastic, you could compare similar products, shop around, or wait for a better price.

First, you might do some comparison shopping. Chances are that more than one place (both in stores and online) carry the kind of product that you want. By comparing similar products and choosing the one with the best value, you can save money. (But remember that ordering online means that you might have shipping costs.)

Next, look for sales. When an item is on sale, it costs less than its original price. Many stores and online sites also have clearance areas, where items have prices that are a lot lower than their original prices. If a product is not on sale, you might wait a week or two to see if it goes on sale in any stores in your area.

Running your own business

Now it is your turn to figure out how supply and demand affects you. Returning to the idea of a cookie business mentioned on page 7, let's say you are in a baking mood and figure that you can make money. You decide to start your own cookie business.

What goes in

You check out cookie recipes online and find an easy one for shortbread cookies. It only has three ingredients: flour, butter, and sugar. These items are also called your raw materials.

What is it going to cost?

Next, you have to think about your costs. First of all, you have fixed costs. You will have to buy a cookie sheet, which costs $10. Fortunately, you already have an oven in your kitchen, but in the real world, you would have to pay for the kitchen, the ovens, and the electricity to run the ovens. With just the cookie sheet to buy, your fixed costs are $10. Next, you have to buy the ingredients. So, you run down to the store and find out that a bag of flour costs $3, a bag of sugar costs $2, and a pound of butter is $1.50.

Figuring out costs

How much does it cost to make one cookie? You have to break it down.

Raw material	Cost of raw material (per pound)	Cost of raw material (per ounce)	Amount of raw material needed for 12 cookies	Cost of raw material to make 12 cookies
Flour	60 cents	About 4 cents	6 ounces	24 cents
Sugar	40 cents	About 3 cents	2 ounces	6 cents
Butter	$1.50	About 9 cents	4 ounces	36 cents

Now, how much does it cost you (outside of your fixed costs) to make one cookie? Just add the costs in the last column to get 66 cents, and divide by 12 cookies to get your answer: 5.5 cents. This is your marginal cost—the cost of making one more cookie.

Ingredients for shortbread cookies

6 ounces (170 g) flour

4 ounces (115 g) butter

2 ounces (60 g) sugar

The right price

Assume that cookies are sold by the dozen. You know the marginal cost of making one dozen more cookies is 66 cents. But what is your price? Remember that whatever price you chose, you want it to cover your costs and then make a profit on top of that.

- ✓ If you charge 50 cents per dozen cookies, then you could not pay your costs, and you would lose money.

- ✓ If you charge 66 cents per dozen cookies, then you cover your marginal costs (the ingredients), but not your fixed costs (the cookie sheet).

- ✓ If you charge $1 per dozen cookies, you will make 34 cents per dozen. You will have to sell 30 dozen cookies before you have paid off your $10 in fixed costs, and the rest is profit.

- ✓ If you charge $2 per dozen cookies, you will make $1.34 per dozen, and will only need to sell 8 dozen cookies to pay off your fixed costs. However, that price may be too high to sell any cookies!

In the end, you decide to charge $1 per dozen. That is high enough to pay your costs, but not so high that you scare away your customers.

Open for business

You set up an old table on your driveway and charge $1 per dozen. You sell 36 dozen, taking in $36. Of that, $23.76 goes to paying your marginal costs (ingredients) and $10 goes to your fixed costs (cookie sheet). You only have $2.24 left over. However, tomorrow you can sell more. Plus, you have paid the fixed costs, so you will make more profit next time!

Business Organizations

What if you wanted to expand your cookie business into a cookie empire? You would need a lot of money to build your new company, and you would also be taking on a lot more **risk**, meaning there is a chance things could turn out in an unexpected way. There are several ways you could set up your business, depending on how much risk you are willing to take and how much profit you want to keep for yourself.

Sole proprietorship

A **sole proprietorship** is one type of business organization. It is owned by one person. Your cookie stand was a sole proprietorship. You made all the business decisions yourself, including figuring out price and quantity. You also paid all the expenses, earned all the revenues, and kept all the profit.

Being in charge of price and quantity and keeping all the profits are positives of a sole proprietorship. But there are also negatives, like having to pay all the costs yourself. And what would have happened if you did not sell any cookies? You would have paid for the ingredients, but you would not have earned any revenue. The bottom line is that you would have lost your money.

A person who runs a sole proprietorship is legally responsible to pay all the money that the business owes. If a business borrows money from a bank, then the business owner owes the amount borrowed plus **interest** (the cost of borrowing money). Even if the business is not selling its goods, or earning enough revenue to cover its costs, the owner still owes this money.

Partnership

What happens if you opened up a cookie stand with a friend? You would share the profits, the costs, and the business decisions. If you and your friend decided to **invest** (contribute) 50 percent each in the business, then each of you would be responsible for half the costs. You might also decide to split the profits in half. A **partnership** has its drawbacks—you make less money, since you have to share the profits. But you also lose less money if the business is not a success.

And what if you wanted to make more cookies? Or if you wanted to open up another cookie stand in a new location? Having a partner gives you more resources, since you can both provide money for expenses or time to bake.

Partnerships are about working together. Many partnerships, especially in banking, have more than 100 partners.

Your partner can also bring other assets, or things of value, to the company. For example, your partner may bring her good reputation or certain skills. Maybe your partner is artistic and can paint signs or make fliers to advertise your business.

Because having a partner brings more value to your business, it may now be easier to obtain a loan from a bank. When people need more money than they have in their bank accounts, they borrow money from banks to start or expand their companies. But just as with a sole proprietorship, partners are responsible for money owed by the company.

Corporations

Having a partner will allow you to expand your cookie company. But what if you wanted to make your business even bigger? You might start a **corporation**. A corporation is a company that is owned by a group of people or by another company. Just like an individual person, a corporation can buy things, sell them, borrow money, make legal contracts, produce goods and services, and even sue someone.

One of the benefits of a corporation is that each owner is only responsible for the money that he or she invests in the company. For example, let's say you invest $100 in a corporation. A year later, this company goes **bankrupt**. This means that it cannot legally pay back the money that it owes. In this case, you would lose your $100, but you would not be responsible for all the corporation's financial problems.

Growing businesses

Is bigger always better? No, but there are many good things about being a large company.

Division of labor

Have you ever been on a team? There are sports teams, school or community clubs, and even groups for school projects. If you were on a soccer team, would you play every position? Would it make sense to score goals and play goalie at the same time? No. Teamwork is about sharing the responsibilities and the fun. It also encourages people to specialize and focus on what they do best.

There are a lot of team players in a big company. And businesses divide the work among them. The idea of dividing up work among employees is called division of labor. (*Labor* is another word for "work.") This division allows people to focus on their strengths, rather than expecting everyone to do everything.

The idea of division of labor is used to make cars. There are many different people who work to plan, design, and put the cars together.

Stocks, or shares, are a type of investment. They are bought and sold on stock exchanges around the world.

Investors

One of the biggest advantages of forming a corporation is the ability to raise a lot of money, which helps build a business. Corporations can keep businesses growing through more than just the sale of products. They can also receive a lot of money from **investors**. Investors are people who put money into something, in the hope of making more money.

These investors can become part-owners of the company by buying **stocks**, or shares, in a corporation. Large corporations offer a lot of stocks. Investors can also lend the money to the company in the form of a **bond**, a kind of investment that earns interest.

WHAT IT MEANS TO ME   **Making money from stocks**

How can you make money by investing in a corporation?

1. By receiving **dividends**: Many companies pay dividends. A dividend is a part of a company's profits that is given to the stockholders.

2. By selling your stock: If you bought a stock for $5 and it rose in value to $15, then you could make a $10 profit if you sold the stock. And the more stocks you own, the more money you can make when you sell them at a profit. However, if the stock's price goes down and you sell it, then you lose money. When the stock values drop, many investors hold onto them until their values rise again. But there is no guarantee that stocks will rise, so it is possible to lose a lot of money.

Economies of scale

Economies of scale are one advantage of forming a big company. This means that the more goods you make, the less it costs on average to make each good. When businesses buy raw materials in large quantities, or bulk, they often get a discount. For example, your cookie company may pay only $25 for the 50 pounds of flour, instead of $30. Now, each pound of flour only costs 50 cents. You just lowered your average cost!

Big companies use economies of scale to turn lower costs into lower prices. Often lower prices will make consumers buy more of that good. This will increase the company's sales—and most likely its profits. Economies of scale also make corporations tough competitors. Many small businesses cannot afford to offer such low prices, so people buy from the large companies instead.

Market structure

You can run your cookie business yourself, bring in a partner (or two), or build it into a corporation. The type of business organization that you choose affects the price and quantity of your product, as well as your risk and profits. There is something else that also affects these items: market structure. The market structure tells you how businesses compete for business in the market.

Businesses operate in different types of market structures. A market is where sellers meet buyers to make sales. For example, the housing market includes people who are selling their homes and people who want to buy homes.

Monopolies

A **monopoly** is one kind of market structure. In a monopoly, one company makes a product with no close substitutes. This company also decides the price, because there is no competition. In some cities, garbage collection is an example of a monopoly. It is a service that is run by the government, and it sets a price that the government pays. There are often no other companies that provide this service to offer competition.

Monopolistic markets often have barriers to entry. This means that there are factors that keep other companies from opening up competition. For example, patents or licenses can give a business the exclusive rights to produce a good or service.

Microsoft: Monopoly or not?

In the 1990s, the U.S. Justice Department, along with 19 U.S. states, accused the Microsoft Corporation of being a monopoly. They felt that this computer company was using its market power to "crush its competition," and that its actions hurt buyers.

In 1999 over 90 percent of the desktop personal computers (PCs) in the world used Microsoft's Windows Operating System. To enter the market of Internet browsing, Microsoft shipped its browsing tool, called Internet Explorer, for free with its operating system. Other companies were not allowed to put their browsers on Microsoft computers. Companies that sold other browsers, such as Netscape, had difficulty competing.

Bill Gates III is the co-founder of the Microsoft Corporation. In 2009 he was the wealthiest person in the world, worth $40 billion. Here, he defends himself during a hearing about Microsoft's possible monopoly.

At first, Microsoft was ordered to split into two companies to allow more competition. After it appealed the case, Microsoft was allowed to remain as a single company, but it had to make changes. Among other things, it was no longer allowed to prevent other browsers (the competition) from being used on its computers.

Perfect competition
The opposite of a monopoly is **perfect competition**, which is when many sellers make identical products. No company or buyer is big enough to affect the price, and people just accept the price that is given to them by the market. There are also no barriers to entry, so businesses can open whenever they want, or they can close if they are losing money.

In between
Many businesses are not monopolies or perfect competition. They are somewhere in the middle. For example, there are a few different major car companies—not one seller (as in a monopoly). But they are not identical, so they are not perfect competition.

Lending and Borrowing

When people and businesses need more money, they turn to banks. Banks lend out the money they have . . . for a price.

Loans

People put their money into banks. This is called making a **deposit**. Then, banks use these deposits to make loans. A loan is a way for companies and people to borrow money and pay it back in the future. Usually a person pays back some of the loan each month.

Many people and businesses borrow from banks. People borrow money to buy goods and services that cost more money than they have, such as houses and college educations. Companies borrow money to start businesses and help them grow, including paying for buildings and equipment. When you pay for an expense by borrowing money, it is called **credit**.

Paying interest

When people and businesses take out loans, do they only pay back the money that they borrowed? No. There is a cost for borrowing money, called interest. Interest is the extra money that you owe for taking out a loan. You can also think of it as the price you pay to borrow the money. The amount of interest depends on the amount borrowed and the interest rate. When a loan is fully repaid, a person pays back the borrowed money plus interest payments.

Borrowing money allows the borrower to repay it over time. For example, it is easier to pay for a car over 10 years than to pay the whole cost all at once. But at the end of 10 years, the car owner will have paid the cost of the car, plus the interest payments.

Interest counts

What happens if you took out a $10,000 loan to build your cookie empire, and the yearly interest rate was 10 percent? Or what happens if you borrowed $20,000 instead? And what would happen if the interest rate were 20 percent instead of 10 percent?

Amount borrowed (also called the principal)	Interest rate	Your interest payments (at the end of one year)
$10,000	10%	$1,000
$20,000	10%	$2,000
$10,000	20%	$2,000
$20,000	20%	$4,000

What does this chart show you about taking out a loan and paying interest? The more money you borrow, the higher your interest payments will be. And the higher the interest rates are, the higher your interest payments will be. And, most importantly, this chart shows that when you borrow money, you pay back more than just the money you borrowed.

Choosing the right borrower

Banks earn money by charging interest on their loans. The more loans that banks make, the more money they can earn. But banks only make money when borrowers make their payments. If a borrower **defaults** on a loan, or fails to pay it back, the bank loses money. So, in general, banks try to offer loans that have a good chance of being paid back. The more certain a bank is that you will pay them back, the better your chance is of borrowing money at a lower interest rate.

Subprime loans

From 2000 to 2007, banks and other corporations began making riskier loans to people who wanted to buy homes. They lent out money to people who did not have good chances of paying the money back. This group of borrowers was known as **"subprime borrowers."** Because banks were less confident that these people could pay back their loans, they did not offer them the best interest rates. Instead these people were given loans at higher interest rates, or loans with rates that would increase over time. This gave the banks more payment for the risk they were taking on, but it also made it harder for borrowers to pay back the loans.

When some subprime borrowers could not repay their loans, the banks lost a lot of money. Since banks use this money to make new loans, this meant that banks did not have money to make new loans. People and businesses suddenly had a harder time getting the money they needed from banks.

Between 2000 and 2007, banks began offering home loans to people who had little chance of paying them off.

How interest works

For a lender, interest is money that is earned. For a borrower, interest is money that is paid.

Earning interest

When you keep your money in the bank, you are actually lending your money to the bank. As a lender, you earn money. How much money you earn depends on your **balance** and on the interest rate. (A balance is the amount of money that you have in your bank account.) Higher balances earn more money. Higher interest rates also earn more money.

These are two types of interest: simple interest and compound interest.

Many people get into trouble by owing money to credit card companies. Until you pay back all of the money that you owe, you will be paying interest.

Simple interest

Simple interest is interest earned on an original amount of money that is invested or deposited. If you deposited $100 in an account with a simple interest rate of 12 percent per year, then you would earn $12 in interest at the end of the year.

Compound interest

With compound interest, the interest is calculated on the original amount plus any interest it has already earned. Once the interest has been added to the total, the new total starts to earn interest. If the deposit of $100 were compounded monthly, then at the end of the first month you would have earned $1 in interest (because after one-twelfth of the year, you would earn one-twelfth of the annual rate). The next month, you would earn interest on $101—the money you originally invested plus the dollar you earned in interest. At the end of the year, you will have earned more than $12 in interest.

"The rule of 72"

If you put money in the bank, how long will it take for your money to double? "The rule of 72" is a quick way to find out. Just divide 72 by the interest rate. The number you get is the number of years until a bank balance doubles (assuming there are no deposits or withdrawals). For example, if the bank offers a 2 percent interest rate, then it will take about 36 years for a balance to double. A 10 percent interest rate doubles your money in about 7 years.

Compounding interest

Ruthie has $1,000 and is trying to decide between an account with simple interest and an account that offers compound interest. If Ruthie invested her $1,000 in an account that earned 10 percent simple interest, then she would have $1,100 at the end of the year—her original balance of $1,000 plus $100 in interest. But what happens to Ruthie's $1,000 if she chooses to deposit it into an account that earns 10 percent compounded monthly, or 12 times a year?

MONTHLY COMPOUND INTEREST			
Month	Original balance	Compound interest earned	New balance
January	$1,000.00	$8.33 (one-twelfth of 10 percent of $1,000)	$1,008.33
February	$1,008.33	$8.40	$1,016.73
March	$1,016.73	$8.47	$1,025.20
April	$1,025.20	$8.54	$1,033.74
May	$1,033.74	$8.61	$1,042.35
June	$1,042.35	$8.69	$1,051.04

This compounding interest continues each month. At the end of one year, Ruthie would have $1,104.70—her original balance of $1,000 plus $104.70 in interest. This is almost $5 more than she would earn with simple interest.

Compound interest gives you more money than simple interest, because you receive interest on the original balance and the interest already earned. Over long periods of time, it adds up!

Paying interest

Earning simple and compound interest are examples of interest working for you. But when you are a borrower, interest works against you. Interest is often compounded monthly, or sometimes even more often. For example, if you made a $350 purchase on a credit card that charges a 19 percent interest rate, after six months you would owe the initial $350, plus $34.59 in interest. Many people keep balances of thousands of dollars and end up owing hundreds of dollars in interest.

Risk

If someone gave you $1,000 and a chance to double that money at the risk of losing it all, what would you do? Would you put the $1,000 in the bank? Or would you be willing to risk it all?

If you put $1,000 into almost any bank today, there is no risk of losing your money. Most banks are insured, so even if they fail, your $1,000 is still protected. But if you put $1,000 into stocks and the company fails or the value of the stock drops, you could lose some (or all) of your money.

Bank runs

When you put money into the bank, does the bank keep it safe and sound? No. It lends it out to other people for a profit. However, banks always keep some money in reserve, just in case you tried to withdraw it all tomorrow. But what if everyone tried to withdraw their money tomorrow? Banks would not have enough money. Too much of it is out on loan.

Usually this does not happen. However, sometimes people start to lose confidence in a bank. There might be a rumor that a bank is running out of cash. Soon people rush to get their money out in time. So, even if the rumor is not true, the bank really does run out of money! This happened in the United States during the Great **Depression**, which began in 1929 and continued throughout the 1930s. More recently, in 2007, customers in the United Kingdom rushed to take their money out of the Northern Rock Bank because they believed it would fail.

However, most countries have taken measures to ensure that banks do not run out of money. An insurance plan set up by the banks and government will repay the depositors any money that is lost.

Panicked customers withdrew £2 billion ($4 billion) from the Northern Rock Bank in just three days.

Why do people make risky investments? They do it because they can make more money if the investment succeeds. If you invested $1,000 in stocks and the company's stock went up, you would probably make more money (maybe a lot more money) on your stock investment than you would by putting $1,000 in the bank.

Passing on risk

During most of the 1900s, banks took in deposits and lent money. They remained responsible for their loans until people repaid them. Since banks only made money on loans that were paid back, they tried to make only low-risk loans, meaning loans that had a high chance of being paid back.

Today, the banking world deals differently with risk. **Deregulation**, or the elimination of rules that governments place on the banking industry, has allowed banks to offer more services, such as different kinds of investments and even insurance. These services, which are generally not risky, provide reliable income to banks. This income makes it possible for banks to take on more risk in other areas, such as the loans they provide—in hopes of making more money.

But because of deregulation, banks are now allowed to resell the loans they give. This shares the risk with others, as the problem of taking on someone who might not repay a loan can be passed on to another bank that buys the loan. Again, this helps them to take on more risk in the loans they decide to give. This risky approach led banks to give loans to "subprime borrowers" (see page 23), which brought about an economic crisis when people could not repay these loans.

WHAT IT MEANS TO ME   **Balancing your risk**

Risk also involves balance. For example, let's say you just received $100 in birthday gifts and decided to become an investor. You put $40 into a risky investment and $60 into a safe investment (for example, putting it in the bank). This way, you have a chance of making a lot of money from the riskier investment and a small amount of money from the safe investment.

You also have a bigger chance that you could lose you $40 from the riskier investment. But if that happens, then you still have the money from the safe investment. So, you balanced your risk by putting your money into both risky and safe investments.

Central Banks and Monetary Policy

Most countries have many banks. They also have one **central bank**— a national bank that helps to manage risks to the economy. It can loan the government money and even decide the amount of money available in a country's economy.

Central banks worldwide

There are over 100 central banks in the world. The oldest central bank in the world is the Sveriges Riksbank. This Swedish bank is 350 years old. The central bank in the United States is called the Federal Reserve. Other central banks include the Bank of England, the Bank of Canada, the People's Bank of China, the Reserve Bank of Australia, and the European Central Bank.

What do central banks do?

One thing a central bank does is lend money to other banks and the federal government. It also has the very important job of keeping a healthy banking system and managing risk in the financial world. It keeps an eye on how banks run and makes sure that there is not too much risk being taken.

The Bank of England is the United Kingdom's central bank.

Central banks make sure that banks are following banking **regulations**. These rules control the behavior of individuals, firms, and financial institutions—including how banks carry out their business. Regulations are often put in place to reduce risk. Central banks make sure that other banks are following these rules.

Money supply

One of the main jobs of a central bank is to control the growth of the money supply. Money supply is the amount of money available in the economy at a certain time. The money supply includes money in circulation (including the cash in your wallet) plus money in "demand deposits" (such as the money in your checking account in the bank).

Too much money?

When a central bank puts more money into the banking system, banks have more money to lend out. Then, both people and businesses can borrow this money and spend it. But having more money in the economy also affects its value.

Central banks and credit

A central bank can also put in place regulations that protect individuals. For example, a central bank can set rules about how a credit card company sets its interest rates. It can prevent credit card companies from raising interest rates quickly or without warning.

One recent regulation set in place by the U.S. Federal Reserve was to protect consumers from overdraft fees. These fees are charges that banks make when a person has taken out more money than he or she has in the bank to make a purchase. The bank allows them to make the purchases, but then charges an overdraft fee for each purchase. The new rules prevent banks from charging overdraft fees unless the consumer has agreed to them.

How much something is worth, or its value, partly depends on how many items are available. For example, think of the one-of-a-kind *Mona Lisa* painting. It was painted by the famous painter Leonardo da Vinci and, according to some experts, it is worth about $650 million!

Now, what would happen if there were hundreds of *Mona Lisa* paintings out there, instead of just one? Each one would probably not be worth as much. They might still be expensive—but not anywhere near $650 million.

The same is true with money. The more money is out there, the less value it has. This can be a problem, because when money loses value, it cannot buy as much.

Too little money?

A central bank can decrease the growth of the money supply—or put less money into the economy. This can maintain the value of your money. But putting less money into the economy also affects how much money there is for people and businesses to borrow. If banks have less money to offer, then people and businesses cannot borrow as much money. This means that people and businesses spend less money, which slows down the economy.

Controlling interest rates

Let's say a computer company is selling lots of computers. People are buying so many computers that the company wants to open a new factory to make even more. But the company needs money to build this new factory, so it takes out a loan. How much will it cost to borrow money? It depends on the interest rate. The central bank is in charge of this rate.

The central bank can have a strong effect on what a country's interest rate will be. The central bank can put more or less money into the economy. If there is more money available to borrow, interest rates are likely to decline. So, in this way, the central bank helps to determine interest rates. When a central bank affects money supply and interest rates, it is using something known as **monetary policy**. The goals of monetary policy are to keep prices stable and to promote maximum employment.

How the money supply affects interest rates

Remember that when there is more of something, it often becomes less expensive. One *Mona Lisa* is worth about $650 million. But hundreds of *Mona Lisa* paintings would be worth less than $650 million apiece. This idea applies to money, too.

When a central bank makes more money available, there is more money to borrow. And when there is more money to borrow, it becomes less expensive. As we have seen, the cost of borrowing money is the interest rate. Interest rates drop when there is a lot of money to borrow, and so getting a loan becomes less expensive.

Conversely, putting less money into the economy decreases the amount of money to borrow. The cost of borrowing money rises, so interest rates rise. This makes borrowing money difficult, and a loan more expensive.

Creating jobs

When the central bank puts more money into the economy, it means that people and businesses have more money to borrow. People use this money to buy more goods and services. Companies use this money to make their businesses grow bigger and to make even more money.

Take the example of the computer company that needed a loan to build another factory. More available credit and lower interest rates allow the company to get this loan. The company can use this money to create more jobs. How? The company creates jobs because building a new factory means hiring more people to build more computers.

When people have jobs, they have money to spend. When people spend, they want more goods and services. Companies that make goods and services keep growing to meet the increase in demand for their products.

Fighting recessions

Creating jobs is one of the goals of a central bank, but it has other goals, too. In 2008 the world fell into a financial crisis. Many countries, including the United States, the United Kingdom, and Germany, suffered **recessions**. This means that their economies stopped growing. Businesses closed and people lost their jobs. Millions of people struggled to pay their bills. The central banks in these countries wanted to help their countries come out of the recessions. They wanted to help the economy grow again and create jobs.

Several central banks tried to spur economic growth by lowering interest rates. Lower interest rates reduce the cost of borrowing money. This encourages both businesses to borrow money to invest and people to borrow money for spending. When companies use the borrowed money to help their businesses grow, they create new jobs. And when people buy more goods and services, they help businesses to grow. When people both invest and consume more, that means more economic growth.

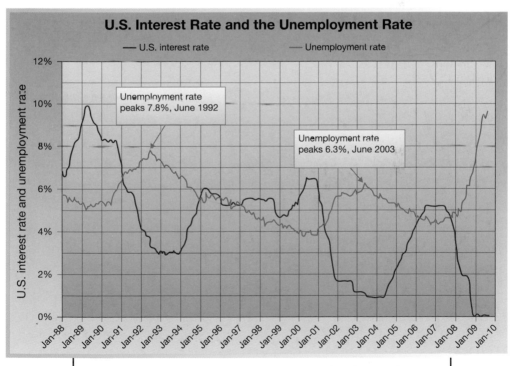

In the United States the Federal Reserve often lowers interest rates when symptoms of recession such as unemployment peak. Unemployment rates often improve as a result.

Buying and selling securities

Securities are investment tools that companies and governments use to borrow money themselves. When the central bank buys and sells these securities, it affects the amount of money in the banking system.

For example, when a central bank buys securities, it puts more money into the banks and lowers interest rates. And when there is more money to lend and it becomes less expensive to get a loan, then more people and businesses borrow money.

But when a central bank sells securities, it removes money from the banks and raises interest rates. This leads to less money for people and businesses to borrow. It also makes borrowing money more expensive. As a result, people and businesses spend less money.

Inflation

If putting more money into the economy helps it grow, why don't central banks keep increasing the money supply? Then, you might think, companies would grow, people would spend, and the economy would benefit.

But increasing the money supply can cause problems. It makes it difficult for central banks to make sure a country's **currency**, or money, keeps its value. This might seem like a simple thing to do, because a dollar is always worth one dollar. But over time, that dollar buys less and less if the money supply is increased and the number of goods and services available is not increased as fast. For example, it takes more dollars to buy a movie ticket today than it did 10 years ago (see chart at right). This general rise in the price of goods is called **inflation**. Economists figure out inflation by comparing the prices of commonly used goods and services, such as milk, toys, and a doctor's visit, from one time to another time.

PRICE FOR A MOVIE TICKET	
Year	Price
1945	$0.35
1965	$1.01
1975	$2.05
1985	$3.55
1995	$4.35
2000	$5.39
2005	$6.41
2009	$7.50

Inflation is usually occurring, but slowly. When it happens quickly, it hurts the economy. This is because the value of the money earned is dropping. Many countries, including the United Kingdom, Canada, Australia, Israel, and Korea, set targets for the level of inflation they want. This means their central banks try to keep their prices from rising to levels that decrease their money's value by too much. The United States does not officially target inflation, but its central bank still aims to control inflation.

Inflation in Zimbabwe

The African nation of Zimbabwe experienced **hyperinflation**, or a very high level of inflation, in the 2000s. In 1980 the Zimbabwe dollar was worth $1.25 USD (U.S. dollars). In the 1990s the nation experienced an economic collapse. As a result, beginning after 2000, inflation steadily increased. In 2006 something that cost 100 Zimbabwe dollars at the beginning of the year cost 1,830 Zimbabwe dollars at the end of the year.

The central bank began to print currencies with higher and higher values to keep up with the inflation. By August of 2008 it took 688 trillion (that is 688 with 12 zeroes after it) Zimbabwe dollars to equal one U.S. dollar! In November 2008 prices were doubling just about every day. Finally, in January 2009, Zimbabwe stopped using the Zimbabwe dollar and began using the U.S. dollar instead to control inflation.

As inflation rose, the Zimbabwe dollar bought fewer goods. Small purchases like snacks cost hundreds of thousands—and eventually millions—of Zimbabwe dollars.

Fiscal Policy and Taxes

Central banks are not the only major institutions trying to keep the economy running smoothly. Governments also do all they can to help the economy. They use their own spending and revenue—also known as **taxes**—to keep the economy growing.

The economy's size can be measured by the nation's **Gross Domestic Product** (GDP), which is the total value of all the goods and services made in a country. If the GDP is rising, the economy is growing. If it is not, then the central banks and the government take action to get it growing again. The actions that the government takes to manage the economy are known as **fiscal policy**.

Buying food from a store or a restaurant is part of the Gross Domestic Product.

Taxes

Taxes are the main source of government revenue. People pay taxes to their local, state, and federal governments. People pay taxes each year, sometimes each quarter (four times a year), and when they buy many goods and services.

Income tax

Income tax is a yearly tax that is paid on income earned from working and from profits made from investing money. It is also a progressive tax, which means that the tax rate increases as a person's income increases. So, people who earn more money pay a larger portion of their income.

Property taxes

There are other types of taxes, including property taxes. Property taxes are based on the value of property. This includes land and buildings, such as houses, stores, and gas stations. The money collected from property taxes goes to the local government, such as a city or town. People may not have to pay property taxes on buildings used for religious or government purposes.

Sales taxes

A sales tax is a tax that you pay when you buy a good or service. For example, when you buy a shirt, the total amount that you owe will probably be higher than the price of the shirt. This extra amount is the sales tax. In the United States, both states and cities can charge sales tax. The amount of this tax depends on the location.

WHAT IT MEANS TO ME   **Paying taxes**

Imagine you made $50,000 working as a cook in a country with the progressive tax rates shown in the table below.

For income that was...	people paid this percent of their income to the federal government...
$10,000 or less	10%
Between $10,001 and $30,000	15%
Between $30,001 and $50,000	25%
$50,001 and up	30%

How much would you pay in income taxes? To find out, you would begin by determining your taxable income, meaning how much of your money can be taxed. Most countries have tax deductions that people do not have to pay taxes on, such as gifts to charities or benefits for having a child. After your deductions, you have $43,000 in taxable income. Does that mean that all that money would be charged at a 25 percent tax rate?

No. Your money would be divided up between the first three income tax levels. The first $10,000 you earned would be taxed at the 10 percent rate, for a total tax of $1,000. The money you then earned between $10,001 and $30,000 would be taxed at 15 percent, for a total tax of $3,000. The last $13,000 of your taxable income would be taxed at a 25 percent rate, for a total tax of $3,250.

Your total tax would be $7,250, which is equal to 14.5 percent of your total income. Even though your total income seemed to fall into the 25 percent tax bracket, or category, your total taxes are less because different parts of your salary are taxed at different levels.

Using taxes

Taxes are used to pay government expenses. Governments, both state and national, pay for services such as mail delivery, garbage collection, fixing roads, police and fire departments, and courts. Public schools are also funded by the government. Money earned by teachers, school buildings, textbooks, computer labs, school library books, desks, and school buses are all paid for by the government. In addition to routine expenses, governments may pay for events such as natural disaster cleanups and wars.

Income redistribution

Governments can also use taxes to redistribute money from one group of people to another group. Governments may do this because they want as many people as possible to have enough money to live on. For example, income tax collected from working people may be given to people out of work, in the form of unemployment insurance.

Helping the environment

Governments can also use taxes to affect how people spend money. Lately, governments in many countries use tax benefits to encourage people to make environmentally friendly choices.

For example, the U.S. government offers tax benefits for home improvements—such as installing new windows, doors, and roofs—that meet energy-efficiency standards. People who improve their homes by using alternative forms of energy, including solar (sun) panels and small wind energy systems, can also receive tax benefits. Throughout Europe, tax benefits are given for energy-efficient investments. Many European governments also give loans to companies that make existing buildings more energy efficient.

Solar panels use sunlight to make energy, which can then be used to heat water and produce electricity.

Stabilization

A government also uses fiscal policy to **stabilize** an economy, or keep it steady. Keeping consistent economic growth is an important goal. People want to know that they will have jobs and be able to pay bills in the future. Companies want to know that people will keep buying their goods and services. When an economy keeps growing, both people and businesses can plan for the future.

Governments cannot control everything that happens in the economy. But they can influence the environment in which we live and in which businesses exist. When the economy is not growing, governments use fiscal policy to improve or stimulate it. They can do this by spending more money. They can also lower taxes to give people more of their incomes to spend.

Bailouts

During the recent world financial crisis, governments (sometimes aided by the central banks) spent taxpayer money to "bail out" companies. A bailout is a gift or a loan made to a company that is in danger of closing. The United States and Europe pledged trillions of dollars in loans to prevent major banks from failing.

Governments hoped that these bailouts would save companies (including banks) and the jobs of the people who worked for these companies. They also feared that if these companies failed, then it could affect other businesses and the lives of millions of people. In other words, these companies were "too big to fail." If they failed, they could cause the whole financial system to collapse.

But these bailouts mean more debt for the governments, which will need to find a way to recover that money—possibly by raising taxes or cutting spending on services.

Deficits and debts

If government spending helps the economy grow, why don't governments just spend money and keep the economy stable? The answer is because governments often take in less money than they spend—usually a lot less! When people spend more money than they have, they go into **debt**, meaning they owe money. Governments go into debt, too. A **deficit** is the amount that a government overspends in a year. Government debt is all the deficits added together.

Most countries in the world are in debt. Since September 28, 2007, the U.S. debt has increased by $3.89 billion a day. If a country's debt grows too high, some people fear that the country will be unable to repay its loans, and other countries and individuals will no longer be willing to lend it money. In fact, this has happened to smaller countries. In October 2008 the country of Iceland's debt grew too high due to risky investments. It declared bankruptcy, admitting that it could not repay all its debts.

Economic Systems

In some countries, the government goes even further than just trying to stabilize the economy. It makes the decisions about how many goods and services are made, what their prices are, and who can buy these products.

Planned economies

Planned economies often go with socialist or **communist** forms of government. In a socialist system, the government controls the things needed to produce goods and services, including money and land. Communism is a form of socialism. Communism occurs when the government plans and controls the economy, doing away with private property and instead supporting common ownership of goods.

The Soviet Union was a major example of a communist country for decades, before its economy collapsed in the late 1980s. It had a planned economy. Today, China, North Korea, and Cuba are still communist countries with planned economies, although China has been experimenting with **capitalism** (see pages 40 and 41) in recent years.

Ownership

In a planned economy, a government controls how goods are produced. Most companies and their resources are under government control. Many key industries, such as railroads and steel production, are also nationalized, meaning they are completely owned by the government.

Promoting goals

In a planned economy, a government can pursue its goals directly. For example, in other types of economies, companies have choices about how to use their profits. But in a planned economy, a government chooses how businesses use their profits. The government can tie these choices to its goals—such as stabilizing the economy by **reinvesting** profits.

Despite having direct control of businesses and their resources, governments with planned economies often do not meet their economic goals. And even when goals are met, many of the people do not benefit. In fact, planned economies usually have economic problems such as not enough goods and services, few product choices, and poorly made goods.

China's planned economy

In 1949 China became the People's Republic of China, and by the early 1950s the government wanted to change China from an economy based on farming to an economy of new and growing businesses. But new companies need capital, including money and equipment. So, the Chinese government lowered interest rates to reduce the cost of borrowing money. This made it possible for people to borrow money to start businesses.

The Chinese government wanted to keep down other costs of running a business, too. So, the government set low workers' wages. This made labor costs inexpensive, but it also meant that workers did not earn much money. To help workers afford basic needs such as food and medical treatment, the government kept the prices of these goods and services low, too. Low costs allowed companies to earn more profits, which were reinvested to help the companies grow even more. China's economy grew rapidly.

In 1958 a leader named Mao Zedong put a plan into practice. The plan was called "The Great Leap Forward." He wanted to increase the number of companies in China and reduce the number of farms. But having fewer farms led to a shortage of food. The government used the food that China did have to feed the people in the cities, not on the farms. It sold the rest to other countries for money. As a result, 30 million Chinese people starved to death.

By 1979 China began to change from a planned economy to a **free market economy** (see pages 40 and 41), though its government has continued to be communist. In recent years, China's Gross Domestic Product has grown quickly. A group called the International Monetary Fund estimated growth of 8.5 percent for 2009 and 9 percent growth for 2010.

The growth of China's economy is apparent everywhere in its busy cities.

Free market economies

The world's wealthiest economies are free market economies. Most industrialized nations, including the United States, Canada, Australia, and countries in the European Union, have free market economies.

Individual rights

In a market economy, most companies are owned by individuals. People own the things needed to make goods and services, including buildings and equipment. They make business decisions such as choosing price, quantity, hours of operation, and number of employees. People also decide both how to raise capital and to use profits.

A market economy structure, also known as capitalism, is usually found in a democracy. Both a democracy and a free market economy are based on the rights of individuals. In a democracy, individuals elect people to serve in the government. In a free market economy, individuals own their own property.

Market determinants

A free market economy is an economic system that is guided by supply, demand, and other market forces. In this system, the buying decisions of consumers drive the economy. This means that the government has very little involvement in the day-to-day working of the economy. The interaction of people and businesses determines market prices and quantities. In other words, the price and quantity of computers are determined by how many people demand computers, and by the amount of computers that companies are willing to make.

Emergence of free market economies

From 1945 to 1991, the large country known as the Soviet Union (which included the modern-day Russian Federation) was taking over countries and making them communist. Its borders grew to absorb 15 countries, including Armenia, Latvia, and the Ukraine. The Soviets also formed a close relationship with countries that included Poland, Hungary, East Germany, and Romania.

Planned economies operated in these regions. But in the late 1980s, the Soviet economy fell apart. At this time the Soviet leader, Mikhail Gorbachev, sent government officials to the United States and to Europe to find out more about a free market economy. After the collapse of the Soviet Union in 1991, borders were redefined and new countries emerged. Nations that were once communist could now decentralize their economies and move toward a free market model.

The invisible hand

Remember that economics involves making choices about how to use limited resources. Adam Smith, the founder of modern economics, believed that a free market economy finds the best way to use these resources and also to give out goods and services. He did not believe in planned economies, but said that some government intervention may be needed to provide services, such as defense.

Today, governments are more involved in the economy than Smith thought they would be. They provide services such as education, health care, and building roads. Governments (and central banks) also create regulations for how businesses carry out their activities. So, countries that are called "free market" are not pure free markets. But market forces still drive most of their economic activity.

It pays to be free

A "standard of living" refers to how comfortable people are in terms of the things they can buy and own. Comparative studies have shown that standards of living are higher in free market economies than in planned economies. In 1950 China, Taiwan, and East and West Germany had about the same standards of living. China and East Germany were planned economies. Taiwan and West Germany were free market economies. By 1989 the free market economies had standards of living that were five times higher than the planned economies.

This map shows the Gross Domestic Product per capita (per person) for countries around the world. The wealthiest countries, in purple, include the world's largest free market economies.

GDP (nominal) Per Capita

International Trade

These days it seems as though just about anything can be bought and sold. That is probably true. However, a country only has a limited number of things to sell. To get those things that a country cannot create itself, or to increase the amount of available products, a country trades.

The wealth of nations

There are a few ways a country can build wealth. It can grow plants and raise animals to use for food and other products. If a country has natural resources, such as oil, coal, or gold, it can use or trade them. It can turn materials into products using industrial technologies, such as turning steel into a car. Finally, a country can build wealth by providing services to others, such as legal services, housekeeping, nursing, or advertising. But how does a country get the resources, food, products, and services it does not produce for itself? It trades for them.

Exports and imports

Exports are goods and services that a country sells to other countries. **Imports** are goods and services that a country buys from other countries. For example, when people in the United States buy cars from Japanese companies, the United States is importing cars and Japan is exporting cars.

According to the International Maritime Organization, over 90 percent of world trade is carried by ships.

WHERE DO THEY COME FROM?		
Apple Computers and iPods	developed in	the United States
Honda and Toyota cars	developed in	Japan
Many toys	made in	China
Financial services and *Harry Potter*	developed in	the United Kingdom
Biggest exporter of oil	is	Saudi Arabia
Biggest exporter of coffee beans	is	Brazil
Biggest exporter of bananas	is	Ecuador

Why do countries trade?

Trade takes place between countries for different reasons. First, conditions, such as climate, make some countries or regions more likely to produce particular goods. For example, tropical climates are known for their production of fruits, including bananas, coconuts, and papayas. Second, companies may choose to find buyers in other countries in order to sell more of their products. Third, consumer tastes can encourage trade. Buyers in one country may prefer the goods produced in another country.

When a country is exporting more goods and services than it is importing, then the country has a trade surplus. And when a country is buying more from other countries than it is selling to them, then the country has a trade deficit.

Having an advantage

A country often exports goods and services that it has an advantage in making. For example, a country may make cars faster or less expensively than other countries. This may happen because the country best uses its resources to make cars, instead of other goods and services.

In the United States, a man named Eli Whitney invented the cotton gin in 1793. Cotton is used to make clothing, as well as furniture coverings and drapes. During this time, many people demanded cotton, which was being made in different countries around the world. But cotton was very expensive because separating the seed from the cotton fibers was hard work.

Whitney's cotton gin lowered the price of producing cotton, and the amount of cotton produced in the United States doubled every 10 years after 1800. Because of Whitney's invention, the United States had an advantage in producing cotton. By 1850 the United States was supplying 75 percent of the world's cotton.

Trade barriers

When countries trade without any restrictions, it is called **free trade**. There are a lot of benefits to free trade, including bigger selections of goods and services, and the availability of foreign goods that can cost less than similar products made at home. However, despite these benefits, some countries block trade.

Tariffs

A **tariff** is a tax that is put on each good imported into the country. A tariff makes an imported good more expensive. Since most goods are elastic in terms of price, tariffs make consumers less willing to buy the imported goods. It may also make consumers more willing to buy similar goods made at home. For example, if the United States imposed a tariff on Japanese cars, then Americans may be more willing to buy U.S. cars, because the tariff makes Japanese cars more expensive.

Trading tariffs

In the first seven months of 2009, the United States bought $1.3 billion worth of tires from China. Chinese tire makers were selling tires in the U.S. market at lower prices than they were charging in China. Since Americans were buying Chinese-made tires, this meant they were buying fewer U.S.-made tires. U.S. tire companies were not making as much money and did not need as many workers.

U.S. President Barack Obama responded by putting tariffs on Chinese passenger and light truck tires. China called the tariff "a serious act of trade protectionism." China also responded by imposing its own tariffs on both car products and chicken products made in the United States.

Reasons for tariffs

Some governments impose tariffs to earn revenue, because the government receives the money from the price increase. The Progressive Policy Institute estimates that the U.S. government earns $20 billion a year in tariff revenues.

There are other reasons for trade barriers, too. Governments block trade to remain self-sufficient or for national security. For example, a country may not want to be dependent on other countries to provide basic needs for its citizens, such as food.

Sometimes a government will also use tariffs to protect a new industry from competition, until it is strong enough to compete with foreign industries. For example, if a country is developing a car industry, it may impose tariffs on cars coming in from foreign countries. This would encourage people to buy the cars made at home, since they are less expensive. It would also give the car industry at home time to build itself up to face foreign competition.

Subsidies

Another way a government can affect the number of exports and imports of certain products is to offer **subsidies**, or payments to local producers of those products. Because of these subsidies, the producers have extra income to live off of. They can therefore afford to charge a lower price for the products they sell. These low prices give them an advantage over foreign competition. The U.S. government, for example, gives subsidies to farmers for producing certain crops. Other countries complain that these subsidies prevent their farmers from getting a chance to compete in the U.S. marketplace.

Quotas

A **quota** is another type of trade barrier. It sets a limit on the quantity of goods imported. A prohibitive quota is a type of quota that does not allow any of the imported good to enter the country. Unlike a tariff, a quota does not provide revenue for the government.

Economic sanctions

Economic **sanctions** occur when a country restricts, or does not allow, international trade and other business for political reasons. These sanctions may include tariffs and quotas. Economic sanctions have been imposed on countries that carry out inhumane treatment of their citizens, engage in nuclear testing, or have invaded other countries.

> The International Development Research Centre reported that agricultural subsidies to developing countries amounted to more than $1 billion Canadian dollars a day in 2003.

Different currencies

Each country, or region, has its own money. If you have ever traveled to a foreign country, chances are that you changed your domestic money into foreign currency.

Currency is used to pay for goods and services. There are about 150 currencies in the world. Some of the more popular currencies include the U.S. dollar, the British pound, the Canadian dollar, the Australian dollar, the European Union's Euro, and the Japanese Yen. Each currency has its own value inside the country itself.

Exchange rates

Exchange rates, like interest rates, are prices. Each exchange rate describes how much of one country's currency can be exchanged for another country's currency. For example, on September 25, 2009, one U.S. dollar was worth .67920 Euros. If a person wanted to buy a good that cost 10 Euros, then it would also cost $14.72 USD.

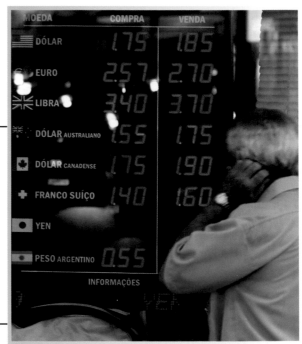

When visiting another country, you can buy foreign currency from a trader. There are two prices listed—the price at which you buy currency (the ask price) and the price at which you can sell currency back (the bid price). The ask price is more than the bid price.

WHAT IT MEANS TO ME   **Strong currency**

How much your country's currency is worth affects you. Let's say the value of your country's currency rises compared to the Japanese currency, the yen. Then, assuming free trade, the goods imported from Japan become less expensive for you to buy. And if you traveled to Japan, the value of your money would be high. A strong currency increases your purchasing power and gives you a greater selection of relatively inexpensive goods and services.

Some countries have floating exchange rates, with values that change constantly. Other countries have fixed exchange rates, which are rates that are set and maintained by the government. When the value of a currency rises compared to the currency of another country, it is appreciating, or becoming stronger. And when the value of a currency falls compared to the currency of another country, it is depreciating, or weakening.

Track exchange rates

You can find out the exchange rate of your country's currency online at finance.yahoo.com/currency.

Floating rates

The United States, Australia, and Canada have floating exchange rates. The rates are determined by the supply and demand for the currency. Currencies are bought and sold on the foreign exchange rate market (FOREX). The FOREX is the largest marketplace in the world, trading almost $2 trillion of currency in 2009— each day!

The supply of currency is determined by a country's purchase of foreign goods, services, and securities. So, as Americans buy oil from Mexico or Saudi Arabia, they pay using dollars, and the flow of these dollars into the world markets changes the supply of dollars. Increasing the money supply lowers the value of money, and decreasing the money supply can raise its value. The demand for currency comes from several factors.

- How people expect their country's economy to do in the future affects demand. A low level of confidence, or expectations, about a country's future economic performance can lower a currency's value.

- If an economy has a rise in inflation, then the country's goods become more expensive. This will reduce the demand for this country's goods both at home and as exports to foreign countries, as people do not want to pay high prices. Reduced demand can also reduce the demand for the country's currency, which causes the currency to depreciate, or lose value.

- Finally, interest rates play an important role in the demand for money. Interest rates are the cost of borrowing money. On the flip side, they also determine how much people earn by lending money. For some investments, the money earned is the interest payment. So, if interest rates in the United States rise, then both domestic and foreign investors will earn more money by putting their money in U.S. banks and U.S. investment tools, such as bonds. This increase in the demand for the U.S. dollar will make the dollar appreciate, or increase in value.

To Sum It Up

You are part of the economy. When you buy something, such as a slice of pizza or a concert ticket, you are a consumer. If you make something to sell, such as cookies, then you are a producer. The houses, stores, restaurants, banks, and schools nearby are also part of the economy.

People buy goods and services, and businesses make these products. But resources are limited, so everyone has to make choices. Economics is the study of how people, businesses, and industries make these choices.

Supply and demand

Businesses supply goods and services, and consumers demand them. Price is related to both supply and demand, but in different ways. Companies are willing to supply more products when prices are higher, because they can make more money. Consumers demand more products when prices are lower, because the products are less expensive.

Different kinds of businesses

Businesses come in all shapes and sizes. A business run by a single person, such as the cookie business, is a sole proprietorship. You make all the decisions, pay all the bills, and keep all the profits (or losses). Partnerships share these things, for better or for worse.

There are also corporations with many investors and many resources. Economies of scale let them make products less expensively. Businesses connect people around the world. A company can provide jobs, goods, and services to people living around the globe.

In the market

There are different types of markets, too. Most markets are somewhere between monopolies and perfect competition. Monopolies have one seller with a product that does not have close substitutes, while perfect competition has many sellers with identical products.

Market structures and business organizations exist in different kinds of economies, including ones in which governments make the business decisions (planned economies) and ones in which people make the businesses decisions (free market).

Expansions

When people buy more products, companies make more products and more money. As businesses grow, they buy more factories and equipment and hire more workers. And people who invest money with these companies (for example, through stocks) also make money. As people spend money and companies expand, the economy grows.

Downturns

When people do not buy goods and services, then businesses do not sell as many products or make as much money. They look for ways to cut costs (like firing workers) and may eventually shut down. These economic downturns are called recessions or depressions. By 2008 many industrialized countries (including the United States, United Kingdom, and Canada) were in recession.

Before this recession, lenders had offered money to subprime borrowers. Many people borrowed more money than they could repay and defaulted on their loans. As a result, banks had less money to lend, and both people and businesses had less money to borrow.

Coming out of downturns

To pull countries through economic downturns, central banks and governments try to encourage people to start spending again. Governments lower taxes and spend money. Central banks lower interest rates, which is the cost of borrowing money. When money becomes less expensive, people and businesses borrow on credit and start spending.

The global marketplace

Countries trade with each other. Trading has many positives. Companies have larger markets, and people have bigger selections and often lower prices. But despite these benefits, governments still impose trade barriers, such as tariffs and quotas, to raise money and to protect their own companies.

Money Through Time

9,000–6,000 BCE	Cattle (including cows, sheep, and camels) become the first and oldest form of money. This is because they can be traded for other goods.
1700s BCE	The idea of a bank forms, as people keep grain and gold (valuable items) in temples for safekeeping.
1000 BCE	China introduces some of the earliest metal coins. The coins often have holes in them, so that people can put them on chains.
500 BCE	The first silver coins are made outside of China in Lydia (modern-day Turkey).
300s BCE	Lending money begins in ancient Greece and Rome.
800–900 CE	The Danes in Ireland slit the nose of people who do not pay the Danish poll tax. The phrase "to pay through the nose" comes from this time.
806	The first bank notes (paper money) are made in China. It will be several more centuries before they become widely used.
1200s	Italy becomes a major banking center. The English word *bank* comes from the Italian word *banca*, which means "bench." Italian bankers do their money lending on benches.
1325–1521	The Aztec Empire uses cacao beans (chocolate) for money. The beans (and their money) grew on trees!
1489	In Britain the first one pound coin, also known as a gold sovereign, comes about under King Henry VII.
1862	The first U.S. paper money, which includes the $5, $10, and $20 bills, is issued.
1930	The world suffers through the Great Depression.
1944	Many countries, including the United Kingdom, tie their money to the U.S. dollar. The value of the U.S. dollar is fixed to gold, at $35 an ounce. This system is known as Bretton Woods.

1946	The first bank card is invented by John Biggins of the Flatbush National Bank of Brooklyn, New York.
1967	Barclays Bank in England installs the first Automatic Teller Machine (also known as an ATM).
1971	Bretton Woods ends and the U.S. dollar is no longer tied to gold. But the U.S. dollar remains the most widely used currency in the world.
	Trading begins on the world's first electronic stock market, called the National Association of Securities Dealers Automated Quotations (NASDAQ). This stock exchange has a large electronic board located in New York City's Times Square that gives financial information 24 hours a day.
1973	Many countries choose to have the values of their currencies determined by supply and demand. This is called a floating exchange rate system. The foreign exchange market (FOREX), which trades currencies, begins to take off.
1995	Over 90 percent of the value of U.S. money transactions is made electronically, rather than by cash or check.
1999	Eleven countries in the European Union replace their official currencies with the "Euro." These countries use the Euro for trading on the stock exchange and for transactions between banks.
2002	The Euro begins circulating as cash.
2005	About 1.5 million ATMs exist around the world.
2007	The New York Stock Exchange (NYSE) merges with Euronext to become a global exchange.
2009	Americans have $972.73 billion in credit card debt.
	FOREX is trading almost $2 trillion in currency each day.

Glossary

balance amount of money in a bank account

bankrupt when people or companies cannot legally pay back the money they owe

bond kind of investment that earns interest; also a security that governments and companies issue to borrow money

capital resources made by people; also, a money investment

capitalism free market economy based on private ownership

central bank country's main bank that can regulate money and carry out monetary policy

communism system in which the government plans and controls the economy

complements two goods that go together

consumer buyer

corporation company owned by many people

credit paying for an expense with borrowed money

currency money

debt money owed

default failure to repay

deficit amount that a government's expenses exceed its revenues

demand quantity of a good that consumers are willing and able to buy

deposit put money into the bank; also used to describe the money itself

depression period when an economy's growth slows severely, during which economic indicators such as average worker income and retail sales decline

deregulation elimination of rules that governments place on the banking industry

dividend part of a company's profits that is given to the stockholders

economics study of how society uses limited resources

economies of scale situation in which producing more goods leads to a lower average cost of goods

economist person who studies how goods and services are made, bought, and distributed

economy system of making, buying, and distributing goods and services

elastic fairly responsive to change—for example, changes in prices and income

expense money that is spent on a specific task, job, or item

export good or service that a country produces and sells to another country

fiscal policy government's use of taxes and spending to affect a country's economic performance

free market economy system that is guided by supply, demand, and other market forces

free trade money exchange between countries, without any regulations from the government or others

good item that can be bought and sold

Gross Domestic Product (GDP) market value of all goods and services produced in a country

hyperinflation very high level of inflation

import good or service that a country buys from another country

income earnings, such as wages and interest from investments

inelastic having a minimal response (or no response) to change—for example, changes in prices and income

inferior good item that people demand less of even when they make more money than they did before

inflation rise in the general price of goods and services

input something put into the production of something, such as ingredients and work time

interest cost of borrowing money; also, the rate of return for lenders

interest rate cost of borrowing money, expressed as a percentage of the borrowed amount

invest to put money into a financial product, in hopes of earning more money

investor person who lends or gives money to some type of organization or financial product, in hopes of earning more money in the future

loan money borrowed with repayment conditions

marginal cost amount that total cost increases with the production of one more unit

market place where sellers and buyers come together to make sales

monetary policy decisions made by a central bank involving money supply and interest rates. These decisions are made to affect a country's economy, keeping prices stable and promoting maximum employment.

monopoly market structure in which one firm decides the price and makes a product that does not have close substitutes

normal good item that people demand more of when they make more money than they did before

partnership business with two or more people that is not a corporation

perfect competition market structure in which no firm or consumer is big enough to affect the price, because there are many sellers, identical products, and free entry and exit

planned economy economy in which the government owns and controls the factors of production

price cost of a good or service

producer someone who makes a good or a service

profit total revenue minus total costs

quantity amount

quota quantity limit on imported goods

recession when an economy's growth slows down

regulation rules that control the behavior of individuals, firms, and banks

reinvest put money earned back into the same financial product (such as stocks)

resource thing used to make and buy goods and services

revenue money that is earned from investments

risk chance that something will turn out differently than expected

sanction government restriction or prevention of international trade and other business, enacted for political reasons

security investment tool that companies and governments use to borrow money themselves

service performed action

sole proprietorship business owned by one person

stabilize keep consistent

stock share in a corporation

subprime borrower person who borrows money but does not have a good chance of paying it back

subsidy government payment to local producers of a product, in an effort to affect the number of imports and exports of that product

substitute good that can be used as a replacement for another good

supply quantity of a good or service that a business produces

tariff tax imposed on imported goods

tax fee charged by the government on items such as income, property, and purchases of goods

Find Out More

Books to read

Allman, Barbara. *Banking* (*How Economics Works*). Minneapolis: Lerner, 2006.

Day, Harlan R. *What Economics Is About: Understanding the Basics of Our Economic System*. Indianapolis: Indiana Department of Education, Center for School Improvement and Performance, Office of Program Development, 1996.

Gilman, Laura Anne. *Economics* (*How Economics Works*). Minneapolis: Lerner, 2006.

Hollander, Barbara. *Managing Money* (*Life Skills*). Chicago: Heinemann Library, 2008.

Maybury, Rick J. *Whatever Happened to Penny Candy?: A Fast, Clear, and Fun Explanation of the Economics You Need For Success in Your Career, Business, and Investments* (*An "Uncle Eric" Book*). Placerville, Calif.: Bluestocking, 2010.

Websites

"A Write to Learn: Money Lessons"
www.awritetolearn.com/money_lessons.htm
What do exchange rates have to do with the Olympics? How can you budget your money and reach your money goals? Find out at this website.

"Don't Buy It: Buying Smart"
http://pbskids.org/dontbuyit/buyingsmart/
Teens can learn how to be smart consumers at this website.

"It All Adds Up: Personal Finance for Teens"
www.italladdsup.org/
Play games and learn how to budget, buy a car, pay for college, save, invest, and use credit cards at this website.

"Federal Reserve Kids' Page"
www.federalreserve.gov/KIDS/
This website provides information on the United States' central bank, the Federal Reserve. Learn about the bank's duties and the way it carries out monetary policy.

Index